To

From

You are the apple of God's eye.

Look on pages 28 and 68
for additional places
to add your friend's name.

Dedicated
to my family and friends...

Michael
Michelle
Gary
Alexis
Jessica
Nancy
Del
Marsha
Jack
Mark
Kathy

whose fruitful lives
nourish and satisfy my soul!

With a special thank you to Nancy . . .
        couldn't have done it without you, my friend!!
And to Mark I am eternally grateful . . .
        for your planting this seed in my heart!!

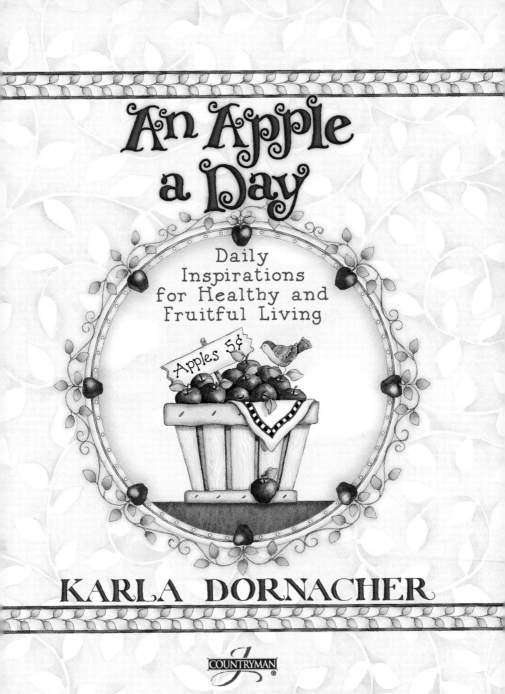

An Apple a Day

Daily Inspirations for Healthy and Fruitful Living

Apples 5¢

KARLA DORNACHER

J COUNTRYMAN®

www.jcountryman.com

Dear Friend,

This book has been such a joy to write and illustrate. Being able to visualize soul~nourishing truths by looking to the common apple reminded me so much of how Jesus taught using objects of nature.

Solomon understood the life~giving properties of the apple when he wrote the proverb, "a word fitly spoken is like apples of gold in a setting of silver" (Proverbs 25:11). He knew that words, especially God's Words, have tremendous power to bring health and healing to our lives.

In this little devotional, I invite you to eat an apple a day of God's golden Word, served in a silver setting of heartwarming, apple~flavored illustrations and stories. As you chew on God's truth and savor the sweetness of it, I pray your heart will be stirred to healthy and fruitful living for God's glory.

In His love,
      Karla

Early in the morning I will rise up and seek Thee.

6

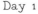

🍎 Today's Apple...

Through Jesus, therefore, let us continually offer
to God a sacrifice of praise ~
the fruit of lips that confess His name.

Hebrews 13:15

🍎 Chew on it...

There is no greater fruit, none that is more
pleasing to God the Father, than the fruit of our
praises. To exalt His name, to sing His praises, to
lift our hands and offer up our hearts, is the
ultimate purpose for which we were called. In
those moments when life is a struggle and our
praise is not found in our circumstances, it is
then that our hearts and thoughts are challenged
to focus only on how great God truly is. It is in
those moments that our praise becomes a holy
sacrifice and we remember that all our
fruit~bearing efforts are dependent on Him
and not us . . . and He gets all the glory!

🍎 Savor the Flavor...

Dear Lord, forgive me for using my lips to
grumble and complain when things don't go my
way. You have been so good to me, Lord.
I owe You my life. I owe You my praise.

Day 2

🍎 Today's Apple. . .

A word aptly spoken
is like apples of gold in settings of silver.
Proverbs 25:11

🍎 Chew on it. . .

Mmmmmmm good! Our words have the power to
nourish and give life or to poison and bring death. God
instructs us to choose life. To speak a word of
encouragement, comfort, or instruction at just the right
moment in time can be as sweet to the soul and as
nourishing to the heart as a gift of golden delicious
apples to both the giver and the receiver. Especially
with sensitive issues, the time and place is as important
as the word itself, so ask God for the wisdom to know
when and where to speak, so the setting will be as perfect
and precious, as the word itself.

Savor the Flavor. . .

Lord, thank You for creating me as a woman of
influence. Fill my mouth with words that build up and
not tear down. Give me wisdom in the timing as well
as the setting in which I speak and let my words always
be a blessing to those who hear them.

God desires to speak golden apples
into your life through the precious wisdom of His Word.
Take a few moments to chew on this verse and then describe
the flavor of its sweetness as it feeds your soul.

"I know the plans I have for you," declares the LORD,
"plans to prosper you and not to harm you,
plans to give you hope and a future."
Jeremiah 29:11

Day 3

🍎 Today's Apple...

You did not choose me, but I chose you and appointed you
to go and bear fruit ~ fruit that will last.

John 15:16

🍎 Chew on it...

You were chosen! Isn't that an incredible thought? Out
of all the wild trees of the field, God chose you, lifted
you up out of the brambles and muck, and transplanted
you into His royal orchard! Now, you've always borne
fruit, but before Christ found you, your branches were
spindly and your fruit was fit only for the birds. But
now that the Master Orchardist is overseeing your care,
you're growing in strength and vigor, and your fruit is
holy and fit for eternity.

🍎 Savor the Flavor...

Oh Lord, thank You for choosing me and giving me new
life in Christ. I don't always see holy fruit in my life,
but I do believe You are working in me and through me
to bear fruit worthy of my King.

A Bushel Basket of Apple Facts

 <u>Fresh picked still the best!</u> Statistics indicate that sixty~one percent of the apples grown in the United States are still eaten as fresh fruit ~ just the way God made them.

 <u>A rose is a rose is a rose</u> . . . unless it's an apple! Apples are actually part of the rose family. So does that make the fruit a giant rose hip?

 <u>The apple variety "Delicious"</u> is the most commonly grown in the United States. Delicious by name . . . delicious by taste. Hmmmmmm ~ good!

 <u>Have you ever heard of bobbing for oranges?</u> How about for bananas? The reason we bob for apples is because twenty~five percent of their volume is air, and they'll always rise to the top.

<u>When is an apple really a banana?</u> Okay, never . . . but in early America the apple was called a winter banana, and there's still a variety known by that name today.

Early Bird Apple Casserole

This is a wonderfully sweet but nutritious casserole~
Perfect for a ladies brunch or get~together.

Preheat your oven to 350 degrees.

Start by mixing 2 cups of sour cream and ½ cup of brown sugar.
Chill until serving.

Next you want to make your French toast for layering:
12 slices of wheat bread
4 eggs
1 cup half~and~half (or hazelnut creamer)
1 T. butter

Soak bread slices in mixture of whipped eggs and creamer. Preheat
griddle with butter and cook bread on each side until golden brown.

Now you're ready to put it all together . . .
12 thin slices of ham (try the maple~flavored kind!)
2 cups mixed, grated cheddar/jack cheese
1 20~ounce can of apple pie filling   1 cup of granola

In a 9 x 13 baking dish, place 6 slices of the
French toast. Add a layer of all the ham.
Top with 1½ cups of cheese.
Add remaining 6 slices of French toast.
Spread apple pie filling over the top.
Sprinkle with granola.
Bake 25 minutes. Top with remaining
cheese and return to the oven for
5 minutes.

Serve with the chilled sour cream
topping and enjoy!!

OH LORD; IN THE MORNING I WILL DIRECT
MY PRAYERS UNTO THEE AND WILL LOOK UP.

PSALM 5:3 (KJV)

Day 4

🍎 Today's Apple...

We do not cease to pray for you, and to ask . . . that you
may walk worthy of the Lord, fully pleasing Him, being
fruitful in every good work and increasing in the
knowledge of God.

Colossians 1:9~10 (NKJV)

🍎 Chew on it...

God has made Himself known to us in nature,
in Scripture, and ultimately in the person of His Son,
Jesus Christ. He wants us to know Him because the
better we know Him, the more we will trust Him. The
more we trust Him, the more we will love Him. The
more we love Him, the more we will want to please Him
and live a life worthy of His love. A life lived for God
will always result in good works ~ good works that will
bear fruit to His glory.

🍎 Savor the Flavor...

Father, help me to know You more today than yesterday.
Teach me to hear Your voice and be sensitive to Your
leading so that my life will not be in vain,
but be abundantly fruitful, bringing great pleasure
and glory to You.

🍎 Today's Apple...

I praise You because I am fearfully
and wonderfully made; Your works are wonderful,
I know that full well.

Psalm 139:14

🍎 Chew on it...

There are tart apples, sweet apples, crunchy and
juicy apples. There are pie apples, eating apples,
bobbing and drying apples. There are about 2,500
varieties of apples grown in the United States and
about 7,500 worldwide, each distinct enough to be
given its own name. God loves variety and that's
why He created you and me ~ similar in some
ways but very different in others. God made us
each unique individuals so that we would bear
fruit to meet different needs. Don't ever try to be
like me . . . the world needs both of us!

🍎 Savor the Flavor...

Lord, I praise You for creating me with my own
personality, talents and strengths. Thank You that
You love me just the way you made me. Help me
to never compare myself to anyone else, but to
use my uniqueness to bear fruit for Your glory.

What makes you different from other women you know? Are you more serious or more playful? Are you more creative or more analytical? Do you like computing more than cooking? List some of the things that make you unique and then ask God to use these qualities to make a difference in your world.

Day 6

🍎 Today's Apple...

See, I am doing a new thing!
Isaiah 43:19

🍎 Chew on it...

Most of us do not enjoy the dormant seasons of our lives, where growth appears to be on hold and the struggles we face cause us to wonder if we will ever blossom or bear fruit again. But it's often during the winter seasons that God is preparing us for whatever He has just around the corner! During the dormant season of the apple tree, it must "suffer" a certain number of very cold days to trigger the development of both leaf and blossom. It's a process called the "chilling hour." During our personal chilling hour when all appears dead, but is not, God calls us to trust Him. We look to Him with a sense of expectation and anticipate the beginning of something new!

🍎 Savor the Flavor...

Dear Jesus, thank You for working in my life even when all appears to be dead. Help me to embrace my "chilling hour" and know that You work all things together to trigger new growth and a more bountiful harvest!

Any fool can count
the seeds in an apple.
Only God
can count all the apples
in one seed.

Robert Schuller

Appleberry Tea

This delicious, fragrant tea would be wonderful served
for a luncheon or any large gathering of ladies.

It's easiest to prepare this delightful brew
in a 30~cup coffee maker.

Simply combine the following ingredients and heat:
1 gallon of apple juice
32 raspberry tea bags
16 regular tea bags
1 quart of water
2 teaspoons of lemon juice
$\frac{1}{2}$ cup of sugar

Just a tip:
Pour hot water into your teapot as you prepare the tea.
When ready, pour out the hot water and fill with the tea.
This will heat your teapot and keep your tea from
cooling before serving.

For fun: If they're in
season, add a couple of
fresh raspberries to
each cup for a
splash of color!

How sweet are Your words to my taste, sweeter than honey to my mouth!

Ps. 119:103

Day 7

🍎 Today's Apple...

A man will be satisfied with good by the fruit of his mouth.
Proverbs 12:14 (NKJV)

🍎 Chew on it...

How easy it is for us to fall into a trap of negative
speaking. When we speak badly about others, it's called
gossip. When we speak negatively about ourselves, we
disagree with the truth of whom God says we are in Christ.
When we speak against our circumstances the Bible calls it
murmuring or complaining. As our ears hear the words we
speak from our own lips, without even realizing it, we are
feeding our own souls with discontent and despair. What
kind of words are you eating? Ask God to help you speak
only those things that are true, honorable, admirable, and
praiseworthy. See if life doesn't start to taste
a little better when you do.

🍎 Savor the Flavor...

Father God, help me to be more aware of the words of my
mouth ~ words to myself and to others. Teach me to speak
only words that are in agreement with Your Word
and bring glory to Your Name.

🍎 Today's Apple...

I am the vine; you are the branches.
He who abides in Me, and I in him, bears much fruit;
for without Me you can do nothing.

John 15:5 (NKJV)

🍎 Chew on it...

Fruit~bearing is essential for us to honor God.
But more important than the fruit itself, is our
relationship to the Lord Jesus as the source of all fruit.
It is only as we are attached to Him,
dependent on Him like a branch is to the tree,
that the sap of His life~giving Spirit is able to flow
freely in us and through us. As hard as we might try,
we cannot live the Christian life or bear godly fruit
apart from an intimate relationship with Jesus.
To keep this vital union with Christ healthy,
we need to take time throughout our day to draw life
from His Word, to stay connected through prayer
and to rejoice in Him through worship and praise.

🍃 Savor the Flavor...

Dear Jesus, help me to draw all that I need from You
to bear the kind of fruit that will bring glory
to Your Name.

🍎 Today's Apple. . .

The seed is the Word of God.
Luke 8:11 (NKJV)

🍎 Chew on it. . .

Have you ever thought about how many apples can grow from a single seed? One seed, one tree . . . but countless fruit! That's how God's Word is! His Word has the power to give life ~ and life more abundantly! From the singular seed of His love, planted into your heart through the power of His Word, God is able to transform your life into a tree of great fruitfulness. You may be only one tree, but your single life has the incredible potential to impact and influence not only those closest to you, but generations to come. Are you letting God's Word transform you today?

🍎 Savor the Flavor. . .

Lord, I want a transformed life. Stir my heart to spend more time with You ~ reading, studying and meditating on Your Word, allowing it to mold and change my life to look more like You.

The fruit of the righteous is a tree of life. Proverbs 11:3

Day 10

🍎 Today's Apple. . .

The fruit of the righteous is a tree of life,
and he who wins souls is wise.

Proverbs 11:30 (NKJV)

🍎 Chew on it. . .

Every day we are given opportunities to offer the
life~giving fruit of God's love to those around us ~ fruit
that has been formed in us, not because of who we are,
but because of who God is in us. God desires this fruit to
be evident in our everyday lives as we reach out and
offer a taste of God's love, acceptance, and forgiveness to
a lost and lonely world through our words and deeds.
This is the fruit that wins hearts to Christ.

🍎 Savor the Flavor. . .

Lord, help me to remember that every act of love and
kindness is an opportunity to offer Your life~giving fruit
to those who do not know You. Let my branches stretch out
in new ways today.

Apple Baskets aren't only for teachers

Great Family or Mom's Gift to start the new school year!
Add some bits of Americana for a July 4th Hostess Gift.
Deliver as a Get~well Gift... an apple a day!
Give as a Harvest Party Door Prize.
As a Gift of Encouragement, include a note saying...
"You are the apple of God's eye!"

Apple Basket Ideas!

Line your basket with excelsior and add a raffia
bow. Start with a few juicy apples and then,
depending on the occasion, choose a few of the
following goodies to finish filling your basket.

A bag of apple chips

Red and green pencils

Sparkling apple cider

Apple erasers

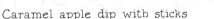

Dried apples in a bag
or on a string

Caramel apple dip with sticks

Apple cider for mulling with a bag of mulling spices

Apple cinnamon tea

An apple decorated teacup or mug

Apple flavored jellybeans

A red and green apple towel

An apple parer

Red and green candles

Apple shaped cookie cutter

American flags

And, oh yes, don't forget a copy of this little devotional
and a note that says, "You are the apple of God's eye!"

Day 11

🍎 Today's Apple. . .

Give her of the fruit of her hands,
and let her own works praise her in the gates.

Proverbs 31:31 (NKJV)

🍎 Chew on it. . .

Dorcas was a woman who loved God, not just in word but
also with the fruit of her hands. She was known for her
acts of kindness, especially towards the poor. The Bible
tells us that when she died, her friends gathered around
her to mourn their loss. When the apostle Peter arrived to
pray for her, these women, mostly widows, proudly
showed him the robes and other clothing that she had
made for them. No one had to try and make up nice
things to say about this woman ~ her own works brought
her honor and praise. But there's more to the story.
Peter prayed and Dorcas' life was restored! God
apparently had more for her to do.

Savor the Flavor. . .

Oh Lord, make me more sensitive to the needs of others,
and help me to be more generous with the fruit of my
hands. Protect me, in my giving, from the temptation to
work for the praises of others or to look for my value
anywhere else but in You.

Day 12

🍎 Today's Apple...

And hope does not disappoint us, because God has poured
out His love into our hearts by the Holy Spirit,
whom He has given us.

Romans 5:5

🍎 Chew on it...

An apple tree is thirsty for water, knowing that the
amount of moisture it receives will critically affect the
quantity and the quality of its fruit. It sends its roots
down deep into the soil in search of life~giving moisture.
The same can be said of us ~ the greater our desire to
bear fruit that is both eternal and abundant, the thirstier
for God we become. The love of the Lord is a fountain of
living water to our souls, cleansing us from our sin and
giving life to those who drink of it. As we tap into this
never~ending flow of grace through time spent in the
Word and in prayer, there is hope for even the most dry
and stagnant places in our lives to come to life and in
time bear abundant fruit.

🍎 Savor the Flavor...

Are you thirsty for God's love? Do you long for the water of
His Spirit to fill the dry and stagnant places of your life?
Are you allowing enough time in your day for a thorough
watering of God's Word and soaking it up through prayer?

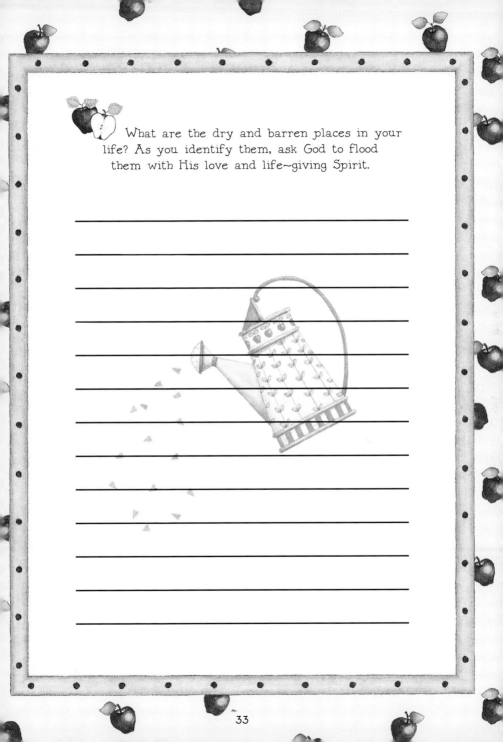

What are the dry and barren places in your life? As you identify them, ask God to flood them with His love and life~giving Spirit.

🍎 Today's Apple...

Blessed is the woman . . . whose delight is in the law of the
LORD, and on His law she meditates day and night. She is
like a tree planted by streams of water, which yields its
fruit in season and whose leaf does not wither.

Adapted from Psalm 1

🍎 Chew on it...

Psalm 1 paints a picture of a woman who is growing by
grace. She has chosen with passion to live according to God's
Word and finds nourishment in His wisdom. She does not dig
her own wells, but draws from the living water of the Holy
Spirit. She is a woman who understands that spiritual growth
is a process and is able to savor the seasons ~ allowing God's
hand a time to prune and a time to harvest, allowing her
life a time of rest and a time to bear fruit. She does not
grow weary, but perseveres for the One she loves.

🍎 Savor the Flavor...

Father, I do delight in Your Word and Your will for my life.
Help me to embrace this season as part of Your plan for my
life and look forward to the fruit I will bear in due time.

The LORD bless you and keep you;
the LORD make His face shine upon you
and be gracious to you;
the LORD turn His face toward you
and give you peace.

Numbers 6:24~27

Apple Butter Blessings

Half the blessing of this recipe is that
it starts with using store~bought applesauce!
The rest of the blessing is in its flavor.

2 cups unsweetened applesauce
1½ cups sugar
1 tsp cinnamon
½ tsp allspice
pinch of ginger
pinch of cloves

Combine all above ingredients into a saucepan
and bring to a boil. Reduce heat and simmer
for one hour. Cool and serve.

How easy can it be!

For a tasty treat, mix apple butter with sour cream
for a fruit salad dressing.

Love is a fruit
in season at all times,
and within the reach
of every hand.

♥ Mother Teresa ♥

Day 14

🍎 Today's Apple...

You will know them by their fruits.
Matthew 7:16 (NKJV)

🍏 Chew on it...

Many years ago, we had only one car. I spent my days
alone with my baby and would often yearn for company.
So when a woman knocked at my door and offered to
come visit me every week I was thrilled. She was
genuinely kind and compassionate and seemed to honestly
care about me as a person. She brought her Bible and we
would study together, but the more I studied on my own,
the more I realized that many of the things she wanted
me to believe did not agree with the Book she gave me to
read. She had an appearance of fruitfulness, but the fruit
of her words did not line up with the truth of Scripture.
How can we know a religious counterfeit? By knowing the
real Jesus and the truth of His Word.

🍎 Savor the Flavor...

Heavenly Father, I believe that every Word that is
written in Scripture has been inspired by You and is
profitable in showing me what is true, revealing where
I'm wrong, correcting my mistakes, and teaching me to
live for You. Always remind me to check the fruit I'm
being fed by others, to make sure it's been taken
from Your garden.

Day 15

🍎 Today's Apple...

He cuts off every branch that doesn't produce
fruit, and He prunes the branches that do bear
fruit so they will produce even more. You have
already been pruned for greater fruitfulness
by the message I have given you.

John 15:2~3 (NLT)

🍎 Chew on it...

Pruning is a promise of God to those who yearn to
be more fruitful for Him. None of us like the
thought of being pruned, though, do we? But what's
the alternative? Have you ever seen an abandoned
fruit tree left to its own? Its branches are
spindly and weak, and the little fruit it produces
is usually deformed and wormy. Like it or not, we
need pruning. God's Word is His pruning tool of
choice, but affliction is often necessary to remove
the dead, sickly or barren branches. The trimming
away of the old branches forces new and healthier
ones to develop, which in turn, allows us to produce
larger, higher quality, and more valuable fruit. Isn't
that what we all want?

🍎 Savor the Flavor...

Dear Lord, thank You that You have not abandoned
me or left me on my own. Help me to be obedient
to Your Word and to not resist the work of the
Holy Spirit as He prunes me to
greater fruitfulness for You.

Day 16

🍎 Today's Apple...

No discipline seems pleasant at the time, but painful.
Later on, however, it produces a harvest of righteousness
and peace for those who have been trained by it.

Hebrews 12:11

🍎 Chew on it...

As a young mom I had no idea how to parent. Not
knowing God, I was prone to discipline out of anger and
frustration, not out of love. I am eternally grateful to
the folks who invited me to see a Christian film that
showed me that true discipline flows from a loving heart
and a sincere desire to want the best for the child
because that's how our heavenly Father is with us. When
He sees attitudes and behaviors in our lives that are
harmful to us and keep us from being all that we are
designed to be, He will allow trials and afflictions in our
lives ~ not to harm us but to train us and make us more
fruitful in days to come.

🍎 Savor the Flavor...

Heavenly Father, thank You for loving me enough to discipline
me when I need it. Help me to understand that
Your correction is never condemning but is always designed
to bring me closer to You.

Day 17

🍎 Today's Apple...

So when the woman saw that the tree was good
for food, that it was pleasant to the eyes,
and a tree desirable to make one wise,
she took of its fruit and ate.

Genesis 3:6 (NKJV)

🍎 Chew on it...

Being a visual person, I dread to consider how many times
I have been lured to sin by what I see. But just because
something looks good on the outside does not mean it will
be a blessing to our lives . . . just ask Eve. She lusted
after fruit that God had not designed for her to have, she
gave into the temptation, and it robbed her of the life and
the blessings God had planned for her. We are tempted
almost every day to want, demand, and take things that
God might not have planned for us to have. Before we just
reach out and pick something, we need to stop and ask God if it's
really His will for our lives at this time. In Eve's desire to
be wise, she should have listened to God. Do we?

🍎 Savor the Flavor...

Dear Lord, help me to ask for Your guidance, to hear and
be obedient to Your voice when You answer. Guard my
eyes and my heart so that I may not give into the
temptation to take hold and eat of anything that does not
have Your full stamp of approval.

There's an angel in my garden,
who watches over me,
I know she smiles as I talk to God
under the apple tree.

Reach for
the highest apple
you can always
get the lowest ones
later!

Anonymous

God bless our home

Savory Grace

Heaven Scent
eau de parfum

Day 18

Today's Apple...

Jesus said, "Feed My sheep."
John 21:17

Chew on it...

Before Jesus ascended into heaven, He told one of His followers
to feed His sheep. He wasn't talking about delicious apples from
a tree, nor was He referring to those cuddly, cute lambs of the
field. Jesus was talking about us feeding one another with the
fruit of our lives. We don't have to be preachers or teachers or
scholars to feed others. We don't have to be rich or pretty or
perfect either. We offer spiritual food by giving of ourselves ~
our words, time, talents, and money ~ in the ordinary moments
of our daily lives. That's how we were designed, to bear
fruit ~ fruit that feeds and nourishes Jesus' other sheep.

Savor the Flavor...

Father, help me not to be selfish with the fruit
of my life. It is a privilege to serve You by serving
others. I release my hold on my time, talents, and
resources that together we might feed Your sheep.

Day 19

🍎 Today's Apple...

Those who are planted in the house of the LORD shall
flourish in the courts of our God, they shall still bear fruit
in old age; they shall be fresh and flourishing.

Psalm 92:13,14 (NKJV)

🍎 Chew on it...

I remember the time I arrived at a retreat and discovered
that most of the women present were over sixty~five
years old. As the main speaker that weekend, my heart
sunk as I wondered how my message would be relevant to
their age, to their season of life. As I prayed and asked
God if I should try to alter the message, I heard this little
voice say, "There is no retirement in Christ!" I gave the
message as I had prepared it and it bore fruit. You see,
we can retire from a job, we can even retire as a full~time
parent when our children are grown, but when we've
been planted in the house of our God, we can never
retire from our call and responsibility to bear fruit! And
the promise is, as we continue to bear fruit,
God will keep us fresh and flourishing!

🍎 Savor the Flavor...

Dear Jesus, our culture sometimes devalues those who are
aging in years but I know You don't. Thank You that we
are able to bear fruit, no matter our age, as we stay
planted in Your presence and plan.

Day 20

🍎 Today's Apple...

This is to my Father's glory, that you bear much fruit,
showing yourselves to be My disciples.

John 15:8

Chew on it...

An apple tree naturally produces apples, just as orange
trees bear oranges and we look for peaches on a peach
tree. When people look at us, they want to see the fruit of
Jesus in our lives. God the Father is glorified when our
fruitfulness reveals the nature of His Son. As we allow
the Holy Spirit to freely flow in us and through us, we
will progressively look, sound, and act less and less like us
and more and more like Him. The world is watching,
looking for our fruit, looking for Jesus in the character of
our lives. Whom are they seeing when they look at you?

🍎 Savor the Flavor...

Oh Lord, thank You for calling me to follow You and
be Your disciple. You know my heart is for people to see You
through me, so show me, Lord, where I still look too much
like me and not enough like You. Give me
the power to change.

🍎 Today's Apple...

Let us not become weary in doing good, for at the proper time
we will reap a harvest if we do not give up.

Galatians 6:9

🍎 Chew on it...

Whenever God calls us to invest ourselves, whether in a person
or a project, if we don't see results in a short time we begin to
question the value of our investment, the outcome, and in a
sense, God's power to work in the waiting. For me, it seemed like
an eternity between my first prayers for my husband's salvation
and his acceptance of Christ eighteen years later. But God
encourages us not to give up but to trust Him, His timing, and
His plan. Keep praying, keep believing, and continue doing good!
The reward will be worth the wait!

Savor the Flavor...

Father, You know where my heart is weary. Thank You for your
strength to keep on keeping on. Help me today to put my
expectations in You and not in others or even in my own good
works, so that when the harvest is ready You will get the glory!

Apple of God's Eye Pie

1/2 cup white sugar   1/4 cup firmly packed brown sugar
1/4 cup flour   1 teaspoon of apple pie spice

6 cups peeled, cored, and sliced tart cooking apples
2   9~inch prepared pie crusts, unbaked

1 tablespoon butter   1 teaspoon sugar

Preheat oven to 400 degrees.
Mix together the white sugar, brown sugar, flour, and
apple pie spice in a large mixing bowl.

Add the apples and toss to coat evenly.

Spoon filling into prepared bottom crust.
Drape the top crust over the pie. Fold the edges of the top
crust under bottom crust edge and crimp together with your
fingers to seal it. Cut slits in the top crust to
allow steam to escape.

Brush the top crust with butter and sprinkle with sugar.
Cover edge of crust with 2~inch strips of foil.
Place pie plate on cookie sheet and bake for 35 minutes.
Remove the foil and bake another 10 to 20 minutes
until apples are tender and crust is golden brown.

Cool on rack. Slice, serve, and enjoy!
Taste and see that the Lord is good!

Core Values

Do unto others as you would like them

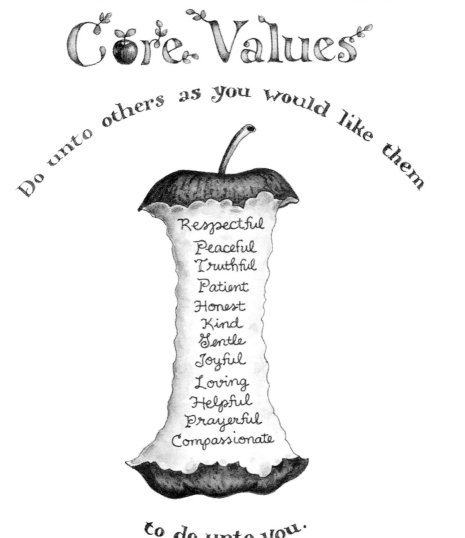

Respectful
Peaceful
Truthful
Patient
Honest
Kind
Gentle
Joyful
Loving
Helpful
Prayerful
Compassionate

to do unto you.

Luke 6:31

54

Day 22

🍎 Today's Apple...

He who sows bountifully will also reap bountifully.

2 Corinthians 9:6 (NKJV)

🍎 Chew on it...

When I plant my garden, if I only plant a few seeds, I will get only a small crop, but the more I plant, the greater my harvest and my joy. This is a basic principle of life, isn't it? But sometimes we fail to apply this principle to spiritual seed. God has filled the seed packet of your life with His love, His blessing, and His provision in order for you to give it away . . . to scatter His seed through your good works. The more you are willing to give, the more He will supply. Take the seed He's given you, no matter how small it seems to be, and generously sow it into someone else's life with love. Look to God not only to replenish what you've given, but to multiply it back to you so you can sow even more.

🍎 Savor the Flavor...

Thank You, Father, for all You have sown into my life . . . I am blessed. Show me the seeds I need to sow today and where to sow them so that others may know how great You are!

Day 23

🍎 Today's Apple. . .

May your roots go down deep into the soil of
God's marvelous love.

Ephesians 3:17 (TLB)

🍎 Chew on it. . .

We all need to be valued, and our natural tendency is
to seek out love and affection to meet that need
wherever we can find it. We often move from one
source to another, looking to people and circumstances
instead of to God. The more we are confident in our
position as a child of God, knowing that we have found
an eternal home for our heart in the very love of God,
the less we seek out other sources for approval and
acceptance. The deeper we put down our roots and
become established in His love, the stronger our branches
become to bear His fruit.

🍎 Savor the Flavor. . .

Heavenly Father, forgive me for looking in other places
for the love that only You can give. Help me to dig
deep and experience the fullness of Your love, so that
out of the abundance of my heart I will bear fruit.

56

Are you seeking your value and sense
of worth in your circumstances or in other
people more than in God? Look up some verses such as
Psalm 139:13~16 or Ephesians 1:3~14 regarding who you are
in Christ and write your thoughts here. Let your roots
go down deeper into His love as you soak up these truths.

Day 24

Today's Apple...

I, the LORD, keep it; I water it every moment:
lest any hurt it, I keep it night and day.
Isaiah 27:2,3 (NKJV)

Chew on it...

God says He Himself is our keeper because we are
His own. He is the One who tends us as His beloved
garden, never trusting our needs to another.
He takes care that we are well watered,
not just periodically but continually, every moment
of every day! And He is our guardian.
His love surrounds those who trust Him,
protecting us from anything that might hurt us.
Our God is not a disinterested, out~there~somewhere god,
but He is intimately involved in the details
of our daily lives more then we can comprehend.
How can we resist His love?

Savor the Flavor...

Heavenly Father, thank You for being there . . . for taking
care of me and meeting my needs in such a personal and
caring way. Help me to be more aware of Your presence,
to trust You more.

Jesus answered, 'It is written:
Man does not live by bread alone,
(*or by apples),
but on every word
that comes
from the mouth of God.

Matthew 4:4 (NIV)
(*the apples are mine)

Health Bites

An apple a day keeps the doctor away!
This saying was around a long time
Before scientists proved it to be true!

~ Diet~Wise ~
Apples are fat free and average only eighty calories each!

~ Heart~Wise ~
Apples are cholesterol and sodium free!

~ Digestion~Wise ~
Apples provide dietary fibers that aid digestion!

~ Nutrient~Wise ~
Apples provide eight percent of the daily vitamin C your body requires!

~ Energy~Wise ~
The easy to digest sugars in an apple give the body a boost!

~ Dollar~Wise ~
Apples are plentiful and easy on the pocketbook!

Day 25

🍎 Today's Apple. . .

But the good soil represents the hearts of those who truly
accept God's message and produce a plentiful harvest for
God ~ thirty, sixty, or even a hundred times as much as was
planted in their hearts.

Mark 4:20 (TLB)

🍎 Chew on it. . .

God wants to plant the seed of His Word in the soil
of our lives, but the amount of harvest all depends
on the condition of the heart. To be able to truly
accept God's message ~ to believe it enough to act on
it ~ our hearts must be humble and pure before the
Lord. We must be willing to surrender our own ways,
thoughts, and wills and want only His truth to grow,
blossom, and bear fruit in our hearts and through our
deeds. The more surrender the greater the crop!

🍎 Savor the Flavor. . .

Dear Lord, please tend the garden of my heart, till
the hard places of unbelief, dig out the boulders of
complacency, and remove the thorns of distraction
that hinder my heart from the hundred~fold!

Day 26

 🍎 **Today's Apple. . .**

But the fruit of the Spirit is love, joy, peace, patience, kindness,
goodness, faithfulness, gentleness and self~control.

Galatians 5:22

🍎 **Chew on it. . .**

You are God's workmanship, and every day He is tending the fruit
of His Spirit in your life. God's fruit, however, has not been
natural to us since sin entered the Garden, and it often takes
suffering and struggles for God's fruit to mature. You see, it's
easy to love someone who loves you, but it takes God's love to love
someone who has hurt you. It's one thing to have peace of mind
when things are going well, but it's a God thing to have peace in
the midst of the storm. It's easy to be patient when you see the
answer, but it takes God's patience to wait for what you cannot
see. You get the picture, I'm sure. God wants us to bear supernat~
ural fruit ~ fruit that can only come as we allow His Spirit to rise
up within us and flow through us to others.

Savor the Flavor. . .

Heavenly Father, help me to embrace Your grace in the struggles
I face today. Show me where my fruit is shriveled or where I'm
trying to develop my own fruit instead of yielding to You.

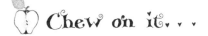 Today's Apple . . .

. . . for they (God's Words) are life to those who find them
and health to a man's whole body.

Proverbs 4:22

Chew on it . . .

Most of us are familiar with the age~old adage, "An apple a
day keeps the doctor away." Okay, so there's no guarantee
about the doctor, but the apple is known to improve one's
overall health significantly. God's Word is even better than
apples! Our minds and bodies are intricately linked together.
When our minds feed on God's truth and our thoughts chew on
what is good and wholesome and praiseworthy, it not only
brings health to our attitudes and emotions but also spills over
to affect the well being of our whole body.

Savor the Flavor . . .

Heavenly Father, thank You for the banqueting table You have
spread before us as we look at the Bible as food for our souls.
Help me to clean out the mental junk food from my life and
eat only what pleases You.

Day 28

🍎 Today's Apple...

My fruit is better than gold, yes, than fine gold.

Proverbs 8:19 (NKJV)

Chew on it...

Sometimes we think that wealth and the finer things in life might satisfy our souls. But God says that the fruit of His wisdom will satisfy your hunger far better than the riches of this world. Are you hungry? God's wisdom is ripe and ready for the picking. It's able to bring God's help and favor into every need in your life. The wisdom that comes from above is pure, peaceable, gentle, and available to all. But you must look up, stretch out your heart and hand toward the heavens to the Tree of Life. Reach out to Him today; take hold of His wisdom and His hand!

🍎 Savor the Flavor...

Oh Lord, I confess I do not know how to handle my life on my own. I need Your wisdom to show me what You want me to do. Help me to listen expectantly for Your voice and to not doubt Your power or desire to speak to my heart and mind.

Apple Cake in a Jar

Preheat oven to 325 degrees.
Coat 8 pint~size, wide~mouth canning jars with cooking spray.
(Regular~mouth jars also work,
but cake will not come out in one piece.)

In a small bowl, mix together and set aside:

3 cups flour	1 tsp salt	2 tsp baking soda
½ tsp nutmeg	1 tsp cinnamon	½ tsp baking powder

In a large bowl, mix together:
2/3 cup shortening   2 2/3 cup sugar   4 eggs

Add to the large bowl 2/3 cup of water and beat well. Slowly add
flour mixture from the small bowl, ½ cup at a time, and mix well.
Stir in 3 cups of peeled and grated apples.
(Try Granny Smith or Winesap.)
Stir in 2/3 cup raisins and 2/3 cup chopped nuts.
Fill each pre~sprayed wide~mouth jar with 1 cup of cake batter.
Bake on a cookie sheet on bottom rack for 45 minutes.
While jars are cooking, heat lids in a small amount of water on stove.
Remove from oven one jar at a time.
Seal each jar with hot lid and ring.

These are very fun gifts!

Cover the lid with a circle of fabric
the size of a salad plate and tie with a ribbon.
Use an attached tag to remind the recipient
that they are the apple of God's eye!

These will stay fresh in the jar
for up to three weeks!

to~
with love

APPLE
CAKE

apples apples ap
pples apples apples apple
apples apples apples

68

Apple Trivia

Johnny Appleseed was born John Chapman in 1774.
Yes, he was a real person who earned his nickname
not only by scattering apple seeds hither and yon,
but by establishing several nurseries throughout Ohio and Indiana.
His efforts provided many pioneers with apple trees
and encouragement as they settled the Midwest.

According to legend, William Tell successfully shot an arrow
through an apple that was perched on the head of his young son.
I always thought he was foolishly showing off his skills,
but tradition says that it was his punishment for refusing
to salute a governor of his time.

Did an apple truly fall on Sir Isaac Newton's head?
It is believed to be true.
Amazing that a falling apple would be the foundation
of a theory that would change the universal understanding
of the laws of gravity!

On a hill stood a tree ~ a symbol of life and liberty

Today's Apple . . .

Walk as children of light (for the fruit of the Spirit
is in all goodness, righteousness, and truth),
finding out what is acceptable to the Lord.

Ephesians 5:8~10 (NKJV)

Chew on it . . .

When we come to Christ, we are transplanted out of darkness
and into His glorious Light. The purity and power of His light
enable us, as His children, to bear the fruit of goodness,
righteousness, and truth in order to meet the challenges of daily
life. There will be seasons though, when our circumstances,
attitudes, or wrong thinking will challenge us ~ hovering over our
heads and hearts like heavy clouds ~ and our fruitfulness will be
affected. But when we desire with all our hearts to please God
and bear healthy and holy fruit, He will not only show us what
is blocking His light, but how to move out from under it.

Savor the Flavor . . .

Father, let Your light shine brightly in my heart and reveal any
area of my life that is not pleasing to You ~ anything that keeps
me from bearing good fruit.

Day 30

 Today's Apple . . .

When the king smiles, there is life;
his favor refreshes like a gentle rain.
Proverbs 16:15 (NLT)

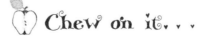 **Chew on it . . .**

It's sad, but true . . . most Christians have never imagined that
King Jesus would smile at them. Have you? Why wouldn't He?
Don't those close to your heart make you smile? And don't you
sometimes smile at people you don't even know? Then why
wouldn't Jesus smile at you? You were made in the image of
God ~ you smile because He smiled first! Close your eyes for
just a moment and imagine Jesus smiling at you. The smile of His
favor will be like a refreshing rain upon your heart. And all of
us fruit~bearing trees need a gentle rain now and then,
don't you think?

Savor the Flavor . . .

Sweet Jesus, sometimes I get so busy trying to please You,
I confess I don't take the time to delight in You
like Your Word says You delight in me.
Thank You for the smile . . . and Your refreshing rain!

Imagine for a moment that you are sitting under an apple tree with Jesus. Close your eyes and look into His face. Can you see Him smiling at you? He is! He delights to be alone with you, even for a moment . . . this is a moment to savor!

Take another moment and write a prayer of thanksgiving to the Lord. Let Him know how much you delight in His smile.

Day 31

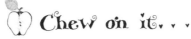 Today's Apple...

Taste and see that the LORD is good.
Psalm 34:8

Chew on it...

I was recently told a story about how every year the graduates of
a particular seminary would come together for their alumni picnic
and an opportunity to hear from a well~known theologian. That
year the speaker, a brilliant man, stood upon the platform and gave
a message that stunned the ears of all who listened as he denied
the claims and deity of Christ. All who were present sat stunned
and silent. Finally, in the crowd, an elderly man rose to his feet
holding a paper lunch bag in his hand. He reached into the bag,
pulled out an apple and took a bite. He then addressed the speaker
by name, saying "I'm not as eloquent a speaker as you or as
educated, but I have one question for you ~ is this apple bitter or
sweet?" The great theologian replied, "I don't know, I haven't tasted
it." To which, the elderly man responded, "Neither have you tasted
my Jesus" and sat down. You will know if you have tasted Him by
the flavor of His love that lingers in your heart.

Savor the Flavor...

Thank You, Lord, for the sweetness of Your love.

A Bushel Basket of Apple Facts

 The smallest variety of apple is the crab apple. The flowers of the crab apple tree are gorgeous! (We just planted one in our yard!)

 October is National Apple Month. That's the month to look for an apple festival in your area.

One of the very first jellybean flavors was apple. I wonder if it was a red, golden, or green variety.

 The apple muffin is the official state muffin of New York! Do you think all states have an official muffin?

Moses Coates patented the apple parer in 1803. Thank you, Moses!

 Over eighty percent of our country's apples are grown in only six states! The state of Washington, where I live, is one of those six.

Apples 5¢

The rose is a rose,
And was always a rose,
But the theory now goes
That the apple's a rose.

Robert Frost

You thrill to God's Word,
you chew on Scripture
day and night,
you're a tree
replanted in Eden,
bearing fresh fruit
every month,
never dropping a leaf,
always in blossom.

Psalm 1 ~ The Message

Dear Friend,

God wants us to taste and see that He is good because
He is! And He wants us to grow, blossom, and bear
abundant fruit because then others can taste Him through
us. I know I want that, and I'm sure you do, too!

I hope that as you've eaten your way through this
devotional and savored the sweetness of God's Word,
that your heart has been nourished and your branches
strengthened to bear abundant and mature fruit . . . fruit
that will nourish others and bless the heart of God!

And I pray that you will always be hungry . . .
hungry for an apple of God's Word every day to feed
your heart and satisfy your soul!

Thank you for allowing me to share my
heart with you once again in such a
delightful way!

For His glory
    and in His love,

        Karla

Other books from my heart and hand . . .

Savor This Moment

Life is short, isn't it? And our days are filled, sometimes to overflowing, with what seem to be just ordinary moments. But each moment we are given is a gift from God, and with the encouragement of this book your seemingly ordinary moments can become extraordinary as you discover God's presence and design in the midst of them. It's a great reminder to slow down and count blessings for all the busy women in your life, including you!

The Blessing of Friendship

Designed to celebrate the gift of friendship, both with Jesus and with other women, this book encourages us to look at the depth and the delights of embracing godly relationships. It includes several journaling pages, which make it an ideal gift to bless and encourage the women friends in your life.

Down a Garden Path

Stroll down the path of a very special garden and pause along the way to let God till the soil of your heart and plant a few seeds of faith. As you read, yield to a bit of divine pruning, or sit in the shade and simply enjoy the presence of the Lord. This gift book is not for your gardening friends only, but for any woman desiring to grow in her faith and walk with the Master Gardener of her soul. Great for new believers and seekers, too.

Love in Every Room

Walk through a very special house where, room by room, you will be encouraged as a woman of God ~ and as the keeper of your home. Excellent gift for a housewarming party, bridal shower, or wedding, or just to encourage a woman's heart.

For more information on my books and gift products
or to share your thoughts and comments,
please write, email, or check out my website . . . I'd love to hear from you!

Karla Dornacher 🍎 P.O. Box 185 🍎 Battle Ground, WA 98604
Karla@KarlaDornacher.com
www.KarlaDornacher.com